Puppy Love

Wiggles and Wags to Warm Your Heart

Free Puppies

Paintings by
Donald Zolan

HARVEST HOUSE PUBLISHERS

EUGENE, OREGON

Puppy Love

Copyright © 2007 by Donald Zolan
Published by Harvest House Publishers
Eugene, Oregon 97402

ISBN 13: 978-0-7369-1802-2
ISBN 10: 0-7369-1802-7

For more information regarding artworks featured in this book, please contact:

Zolan Fine Arts, LLC
Attn: Jennifer Zolan
203.300.7197
e-mail: donaldz798@aol.com
www.zolan.com

Design and production by Garborg Design Works, Savage, Minnesota

Harvest House Publishers has made every effort to trace the ownership of all poems and quotes. In the event of a question arising from the use of a poem or quote, we regret any error made and will be pleased to make the necessary correction in future editions of this book.

Printed in Singapore.

07 08 09 10 11 12 13 / IM / 10 9 8 7 6 5 4 3 2 1

Children growing up with pets they love and care for seem to turn out to be good parents and more selfless mates.

ROGER CARAS

Welcome Home, New Puppy

May I be worthy, God of new beginnings, of this
wee one trotting in my wake. I'm already in love
with this wriggly ball of fur with milky puppy
breath, needle teeth as sharp as exclamation
points, growls that sound like bees buzzing,
and bright button eyes that've taken
my measure in a heartbeat and
know me for the infatuated
fool I am. Bless us as we
explore the world
You've set before us.
Down on my knees in
the wake of a puppy,
O God, is a wonderful place to meet You.

MARGARET ANNE HUFFMAN

If a picture wasn't going very well I'd put a puppy dog in it,
always a mongrel, you know, never one of the full-bred puppies.

NORMAN ROCKWELL

5

Hardly knowing what she did, she picked up a little bit of stick, and held it out to the puppy; whereupon the puppy jumped into the air off all its feet at once, with a yelp of delight, and rushed at the stick, and made believe to worry it; then Alice dodged behind a great thistle, to keep herself from being run over; and the moment she appeared on the other side, the puppy made another rush at the stick, and tumbled head over heels in its hurry to get hold of it; then Alice, thinking it was very like having a game of play with a cart-horse, and expecting every moment to be trampled under its feet, ran round the thistle again; then the puppy began a series of short charges at the stick, running a very little way forwards each time and a long way back, and barking hoarsely all the while, till at last it sat down a good way off, panting, with its tongue hanging out of its mouth, and its great eyes half shut.

LEWIS CARROLL
Alice in Wonderland

The best way to get a puppy is to beg for a baby brother—and they'll settle for a puppy every time.

WINSTON PENDLETON

There's a time in practically every young boy's life when he's affected by that wonderful disease of puppy love...the real kind, the kind that has four small feet and a wiggly tail, and sharp little teeth that can gnaw on a boy's finger; the kind a boy can romp and play with, even eat and sleep with.

WILSON RAWLS
Where the Red Fern Grows

There are times when only a dog will do for a friend...When you're beaten sick and blue, and the world's all wrong, for he won't care if you break and cry, or grouch...for he'll let you know as he licks your hand that he's downright sorry...and understands.

DON BLANDING

Every puppy should have a boy.

ERMA BOMBECK

I talk to him when I'm lonesome like,
and I'm sure he understands.
When he looks at me so attentively,
and gently licks my hands;
Then he rubs his nose on my tailored clothes,
but I never say naught thereat,
For the good Lord knows I can buy more clothes,
but never a friend like that!

W. DAYTON WEDGEFARTH

My sunshine doesn't come from the skies,
It comes from the love in my dog's eyes.

AUTHOR UNKNOWN

A puppy is but a dog, plus high spirits, and minus common sense.

AGNES REPPLIER

All this puppy love was starting to get on my nerves, so I had to make a paradigm shift. One day while walking them through the woods, I stood and watched them frolic—and I do mean frolic: rolling, tumbling, chasing, laughing (yes, dogs laugh), and leaping like bunnies. They were having so much fun, and seeing them that way made my whole body sigh, relax, and smile.

OPRAH WINFREY

The dog was created especially for children. He is the god of frolic.

HENRY WARD BEECHER

The dog of your boyhood teaches you a great deal about
friendship, and love, and death: Old Skip was my brother.
They had buried him under our elm tree, they said—yet this
was not totally true. For he really lay buried in my heart.

WILLIE MORRIS
My Dog Skip

Since he had started playing with his father's hound puppies
a great dream had grown within him. Some day he would find a
dog to shame all others, a fine dog that he could treasure, and
cherish, and breed from so that all who loved fine dogs would
come to see and buy his. That would be all he wanted of Heaven.

JIM KJELGAARD
Big Red

14

Here's my new puppy. Is not he a dear? I'll let you hold him," and she attempted to deposit the fat, curly, satiny creature in Dolores's arms, which instantly hung down stiff...The puppy fell down with a flop, and began to squeak, while the girls, crying, "Oh! Dolly, how could you!" and "Poor little pup!" all crowded round in pity and indignation, and Wilfred observed, "I told you so!"

CHARLOTTE M. YONGE
The Two Sides of the Shield

Puppies are nature's remedy for feeling unloved, plus numerous other ailments of life.

RICHARD ALLAN PALM

Dachshunds are ideal dogs for small children, as they are already stretched and pulled to such a length that the child cannot do much harm one way or the other.

ROBERT BENCHLEY

Perhaps children's innocence, wherever it comes from, contributes to the fact that they seem to see angels more often.

JOHN RONNER

Give a boy a dog and you've furnished him a playmate.

BERTON BRALEY

Every time I told my cocker spaniel, Taffy, my very first dog, that we were going for a walk, she would launch into a celebratory dance that ended with her racing around the room, always clockwise, and faster and faster, as if her joy could not be possibly contained. Even as a young boy I knew that hardly any creature could express joy so vividly as a dog.

JEFFREY MOUSSAIEFF MASSON

You are worried about seeing him spend his early years in doing nothing. What! Is it nothing to be happy? Nothing to skip, play, and run around all day long? Never in his life will he be so busy again.

JEAN-JACQUES ROUSSEAU

In their sympathies, children feel nearer animals than adults. They frolic with animals, caress them, share with them feelings neither has words for. Have they ever stroked any adult with the love they bestow on a cat? Hugged any grownup with the ecstasy they feel when clasping a puppy?

JESSAMYN WEST

There is no psychiatrist in the world like a puppy licking your face.

BEN WILLIAMS

Of all the things I miss from veterinary practice, puppy breath is one of the most fond memories!

DR. TOM CAT

21

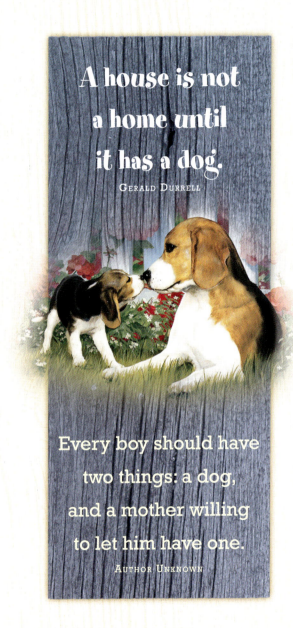

A house is not a home until it has a dog.

GERALD DURRELL

Every boy should have two things: a dog, and a mother willing to let him have one.

AUTHOR UNKNOWN

The next day was a busy one for me. With the hampering help of my sisters I made the little doghouse.

Papa cut the ends off his check lines and gave them to me for collars. With painstaking care, deep in the tough leather I scratched the name "Old Dan" on one and "Little Ann" on the other. With a nail and a rock two holes were punched in each of the straps. I put them around their small necks and laced the ends together with baling wire.

That evening I had a talk with my mother. I told her about praying for the two pups, about the magazine and the plans I had made. I told her how hard I had tried to find names for them and how strange it was finding them carved in the bark of a sycamore tree.

With a smile on her face, she asked, "Do you believe God heard your prayer and helped you?"

"Yes, Mama," I said. "I know He did and I'll always be thankful."

WILSON RAWLS
Where the Red Fern Grows

Whoever said you can't buy love has never owned a puppy.

AUTHOR UNKNOWN

People have been asking me if I was going to have kids, and I had puppies instead.

KATE JACKSON

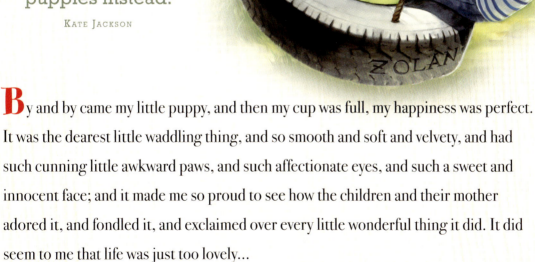

By and by came my little puppy, and then my cup was full, my happiness was perfect. It was the dearest little waddling thing, and so smooth and soft and velvety, and had such cunning little awkward paws, and such affectionate eyes, and such a sweet and innocent face; and it made me so proud to see how the children and their mother adored it, and fondled it, and exclaimed over every little wonderful thing it did. It did seem to me that life was just too lovely...

MARK TWAIN
A Dog's Tale

When you feel lousy, puppy therapy is indicated.

SARA PARETSKY

We give them the love
we can spare, the time
we can spare. In return
dogs have given us their
absolute all. It is without
doubt the best deal
man has ever made.

ROGER CARAS

With eye upraised his master's look to scan,

The joy, the solace, and the aid of man:

The rich man's guardian and the poor man's friend,

The only creature faithful to the end.

GEORGE CRABBE

No symphony orchestra ever played music like
a two-year-old girl laughing with a puppy.

BERN WILLIAMS

It was Toto that made
Dorothy laugh, and saved
her from growing as gray
as her other surroundings.
Toto was not gray; he was a
little black dog, with long,
silky hair and small black
eyes that twinkled merrily
on either side of his funny,
wee nose. Toto played
all day long, and Dorothy
played with him, and loved
him dearly.

FRANK BAUM
The Wizard of Oz

All things bright and beautiful,

all creatures great and small,

all things wise and wonderful,

the Lord God made them all.

CECIL FRANCIS ALEXANDER

29

For just a second Bowser stared in utter surprise. Then with a little yelp of pure joy he leaped up and did his best to lick his master's face. Could you have seen Bowser, you might have thought that he was just a foolish young puppy, he cut up such wild antics to express his joy. He yelped and whined and barked. He nearly knocked Farmer Brown's boy down by leaping up on him. He raced around in circles. When at last he was still long enough, Farmer Brown's boy just threw his arms around him and hugged him. He hugged him so hard he made Bowser squeal. Then two of the happiest folks in all the Great World started back across the snow-covered fields to the sleigh.

THORNTON W. BURGESS
Bowser the Hound

There is only one smartest dog in the world, and every boy has it.
AUTHOR UNKNOWN

Buy a pup and your money will buy Love unflinching that cannot lie.
RUDYARD KIPLING

Love me, love my dog.

JOHN HEYWOOD